CALIFORNIA RULES OF COURT

JANUARY 2025 SUPPLEMENT

An update to be used in conjunction with the 2025 Editions of:

Matthew Bender's *Standard California Codes: 6-in-2*®
Matthew Bender's *Standard California Codes: 4-in-1*
Matthew Bender's *Standard California Codes: Rules of Court*
Deering's *Desktop Civil Practice Codes*

This supplement is to be used in conjunction with the 2025 Editions. This supplement incorporates all changes to the Rules of Court issued by the Judicial Council from November 17, 2024 through Decemeber 15, 2024.

QUESTIONS ABOUT THIS PUBLICATION?

For questions about the **Editorial Content** appearing in these volumes or reprint permission, please call:

E-mail at .... CalCodes@lexisnexis.com

For assistance with replacement pages, shipments, billing or other customer service matters, please call:

Customer Services Department at .... (800) 833-9844
Outside the United States and Canada, please call .... (518) 487-3000
Fax number .... (518) 487-3584
Customer Service Website .... http://www.lexisnexis.com/custserv/

For information on other Matthew Bender Publications, please call
Your account manager... (877) 394-8826
Outside the United States and Canada, please call .... (518) 487-3000

PIN 609999440P

This publication is designed to provide authoritative information in regard to the subject matter covered. It is sold with the understanding that the publisher is not engaged in rendering legal, accounting, or other professional services. If legal advice or other expert assistance is required, the services of a competent professional should be sought.

LexisNexis and the Knowledge Burst logo are registered trademarks of RELX Inc. Matthew Bender and the Matthew Bender Flame Design are registered trademarks of Matthew Bender Properties Inc.

6-in-2 and SIX-IN-TWO are registered trademarks of Matthew Bender & Company, Inc.

Copyright © 2024 Matthew Bender & Company, Inc., a member of LexisNexis.
Originally published in: 1931

All Rights Reserved.

No copyright is claimed by LexisNexis or Matthew Bender & Company, Inc., in the text of statutes, regulations, and excerpts from court opinions quoted within this work. Permission to copy material may be licensed for a fee from the Copyright Clearance Center, 222 Rosewood Drive, Danvers, Mass. 01923, telephone (978) 750-8400.

MATTHEW ◊ BENDER

Editorial Offices
230 Park Ave., 7th Floor, New York, NY 10169
9443 Springboro Pike, Miamisburg, OH 45342
www.lexisnexis.com

Table of Additional Changes

California Rules of Court

Rule	Effect	Date
2.893(a)	Amended	Jan. 1, 2025
2.893(b)	Amended	Jan. 1, 2025
2.893(c)	Amended	Jan. 1, 2025
2.893(d)	Amended	Jan. 1, 2025
2.893(e)	Amended	Jan. 1, 2025
2.893(f)	Adopted	Jan. 1, 2025
2.893(g)	Adopted	Jan. 1, 2025
2.893 Adv. Comment	Amended	Jan. 1, 2025
3.1308(a)	Amended	Jan. 1, 2025
3.1308(c)	Amended	Jan. 1, 2025
3.1385 Adv. Comment	Amended	Jan. 1, 2025
3.1905	Adopted	Jan. 1, 2025
3.2226(a)	Amended	Jan. 1, 2025
3.2226(c)	Amended	Jan. 1, 2025
4.433(e)	Amended	Jan. 1, 2025
5.92(a)	Amended	Jan. 1, 2025
5.620(b)	Amended	Jan. 1, 2025
5.625(a)	Amended	Jan. 1, 2025
5.630(c)	Amended	Jan. 1, 2025
5.630(d)	Amended	Jan. 1, 2025
5.630(e)	Relettered from (f)	Jan. 1, 2025
5.630(f)	Amended & Relettered from (g)	Jan. 1, 2025
5.630(j)	Amended	Jan. 1, 2025
5.632	Adopted	Jan. 1, 2025
5.674(b)	Amended	Jan. 1, 2025
5.676(a)	Amended	Jan. 1, 2025
5.676(c)	Amended	Jan. 1, 2025
5.676(d)	Amended	Jan. 1, 2025
5.678(d)	Amended	Jan. 1, 2025
7.1016(a)	Amended	Jan. 1, 2025
7.1016(b)	Amended	Jan. 1, 2025
7.1016(c)	Amended	Jan. 1, 2025
7.1016(d)	Amended	Jan. 1, 2025
7.1016(e)	Amended	Jan. 1, 2025
7.1016(f)	Amended	Jan. 1, 2025
7.1016(g)	Amended	Jan. 1, 2025
7.1016(h)	Amended	Jan. 1, 2025
7.1016(i)	Amended	Jan. 1, 2025
8.100(g)	Amended	Jan. 1, 2025
8.200(c)	Amended	Jan. 1, 2025
8.200 Adv. Comment	Amended	Jan. 1, 2025
8.320(e)	Amended	Jan. 1, 2025
8.320(g)	Adopted	Jan. 1, 2025
8.320 Adv. Comment	Adopted	Jan. 1, 2025
8.883(b)	Amended	Jan. 1, 2025
8.883 Adv. Comment	Amended	Jan. 1, 2025
10.461(a)	Amended	Jan. 1, 2025
10.462(a)	Amended	Jan. 1, 2025
10.465	Adopted	Jan. 1, 2025
10.469(e)	Repealed	Jan. 1, 2025

TABLE OF AMENDMENTS

Standards of Judicial Administration

Standard	Effect	Date
2.2(m)	Amended	Jan. 1, 2025

CALIFORNIA RULES OF COURT

TITLE 2
Trial Court Rules

Division 6
Appointments by the Court or Agreements of the Parties

Chapter 4
Language Access

Article 2
Court Interpreters

Rule 2.893. Appointment of interpreters in court proceedings

(a) Application

This rule applies to all trial court proceedings in which the court appoints [1] **a spoken language** interpreter for a [2] **limited** English [3] **proficient** (LEP) person. [4]

(Sub (a) amended effective January 1, 2025.)

Rule 2.893(a). 2024 Deletes. [1] an **[2]** Limited **[3]** Proficient **[4]** This rule applies to spoken language interpreters in languages designated and not designated by the Judicial Council.

(b) Definitions

As used in this rule:

(1) "Designated language" means a language selected by the Judicial Council for the development of a certification program under Government Code section 68562[1].

(2) "Certified interpreter" means an interpreter who is [2] **qualified** by the Judicial Council to interpret **in a designated** language **as defined in (b)(1) [3]. A certified interpreter has passed the English written exam and the Bilingual Interpreting Exam.**

(3) "Registered interpreter" means an interpreter **who is qualified by the Judicial Council to interpret** in a language **that is** not a designated **language [4] as defined in (b)(1) [5]. A registered inter-**

preter has passed the English written exam, an Oral Proficiency Exam in English, and an Oral Proficiency Exam in the target language, if available.

(4) [6] **"Relay interpreter"** means [7] **a person who interprets between two non-English spoken languages.** [8]

(5) [9] **"Noncertified"** or **"nonregistered" interpreter means a person providing interpretation services:**

(A) In a language designated for certification by the Judicial Council, without holding a certification to provide interpretation in that language; or

(B) In a language identified as a registered language by the Judicial Council, without holding a registered status to interpret in that language, under the procedures and guidelines adopted by the Judicial Council; or

(C) In two non-English languages, as a relay interpreter. [10][11]

(Subd (b) amended effective January 1, 2025.)

Rule 2.893(b). 2024 Deletes. [1] ; [2] qualified **[3]** designated by the Judicial Council under Government Code section 68560 et seq.:. **[4]** by the Judicial Council **[5]** who is qualified by the court under the qualification procedures and guidelines adopted by the Judicial Council;, and who has passed a minimum of an English fluency examination offered by a testing entity approved by the Judicial Council under Government Code section 68560 et seq.; **[6]** "Noncertified interpreter" **[7]** an interpreter is not certified by the Judicial Council to interpret a language designated by the Judicial Council under Government Code section 68560 et seq.; **[8]** ; **[9]** "Nonregistered interpreter" means an interpreter in a language not designated by the Judicial Council who has not been qualified under the qualification procedures and guidelines adopted by the Judicial Council under Government Code section 68560 et seq.; **[10]** (6) "Provisionally qualified" means an interpreter who is neither certified nor regis-

Rule 2.893   JANUARY 2025 SUPPLEMENT   2

tered but has been qualified under the good cause and qualification procedures and guidelines adopted by the Judicial Council under Government Code section 68560 et seq.; **[11]** (7) "Temporary interpreter" means an interpreter who is not certified, registered, or provisionally qualified, but is used one time, in a brief, routine matter.

(c) Appointment of certified or registered interpreters

If a court appoints a certified or registered court interpreter, the [1] **judicial officer** in the proceeding must require the following to be stated on the record:

(1)–(6) * * *

(Subd (c) amended effective January 1, 2025.)

Rule 2.893(c).   2024 Deletes. [1] judicial officer

(d) Appointment [1] of noncertified or nonregistered interpreters

(1) [2] **A noncertified or nonregistered interpreter may be appointed to provide interpretation services as follows:** [3]

(A) Under a provisional appointment as described in (e); or

(B) Under a temporary appointment as described in (f).

(2) [4] In all cases in which a noncertified or nonregistered interpreter is appointed [5], the [6] **judicial officer** in the proceeding must require the following to be stated on the record:

(A) The language to be interpreted;

[7] **(B)** A finding that good cause exists to appoint a noncertified or nonregistered interpreter;

[8] **(C)** The name of the interpreter;

[9] **(D)** A statement that the interpreter is not certified or registered to interpret in the language to be interpreted;

[10] **(E)** A finding that the interpreter is qualified to interpret in the proceeding as required in [11] **(e)** or [12] **(f), with any other findings required under those subdivisions;** and

[13] **(F)** A statement that the interpreter was administered the interpreter's oath. [14]

(Subd (d) amended effective January 1, 2025.)

Rule 2.893(d).   2024 Deletes. [1] or use [2] *When permissable* [3] If after a diligent search a certified or registered interpreter is not available, the judge in the proceeding may either appoint a noncertified

or nonregistered interpreter who has been provisionally qualified under (d)(3) or, in the limited circumstances specified in (d)(4), may use a noncertified or nonregistered interpreter who is not provisionally qualified. **[4]** Required record **[5]** or used **[6]** judge **[7]** (B) A finding that a certified or registered interpreter is not available and a statement regarding whether a Certification of Unavailability of Certified or Registered Interpreter (form INT-120) for the language to be interpreted is on file for this date with the court administrator; (C) **[8]** (D) **[9]** (E) **[10]** (F) **[11]** (d)(3) **[12]** (d)(4) **[13]** (G) **[14]** (3) Provisional qualification (A) A noncertified or nonregistered interpreter is provisionally qualified if the presiding judge of the court or other judicial officer designated by the presiding judge: (i) Finds the noncertified or nonregistered interpreter to be provisionally qualified following the Procedures to Appoint a Noncertified or Nonregistered Spoken Language Interpreter as Either Provisionally Qualified or Temporary (form INT-100-38 INFO); and (ii) Signs an order allowing the interpreter to be considered for appointment on Qualifications of a Noncertified or Nonregistered Spoken Language Interpreter (form INT-110). The period covered by this order may not exceed a maximum of six months. (B) To appoint a provisionally qualified interpreter, in addition to the matters that must be stated on the record under (d)(2), the judge in the proceeding must state on the record: (i) A finding that the interpreter is qualified to interpret the proceeding, following procedures adopted by the Judicial Council (see forms INT-100-INFO, INT-110, and INT-120); (ii) A finding, if applicable, that good cause exists under (f)(1)(B) for the court to appoint the interpreter beyond the time ordinarily allowed in (f); and(iii) If a party has objected to the appointment of the proposed interpreter or has waived the appointment of a certified or registered interpreter. (4) Temporary use At the request of an LEP person, a temporary interpreter may be used to prevent burdensome delay or in other unusual circumstances if: (A) The judge in the proceeding finds on the record that: (i) The LEP person has been informed of their right to an interpreter and has waived the appointment of a certified or registered interpreter or an interpreter who could be

---

NOTE: Three asterisks (***) indicate unchanged material.

provisionally qualified by the presiding judge as provided in (d)(3); (ii) Good cause exists to appoint an interpreter who is not certified, registered, or provisionally qualified; and(iii) The interpreter is qualified to interpret that proceeding, following procedures adopted by the Judicial Council (see forms INT-100-36 INFO and INT-140). (B) The use of an interpreter under this subdivision is limited to a single brief, routine matter before the court. The use of the interpreter in this circumstance may not be extended to subsequent proceedings without again following the procedure set forth in this subdivision.

(e) [1] Provisional qualification and appointment of noncertified or nonregistered interpreters

[2] (1) When permissible

If, after a diligent search, a certified or registered interpreter is not available, the judicial officer in the proceeding may appoint a noncertified or nonregistered interpreter who has been provisionally qualifed under this subdivision.

(2) Provisional quaification

(A) A noncertified or nonregistered interpreter is provisionally qualified if a judicial officer of a superior court finds the noncertified or nonregistered interpreter to be provisionally qualified to interpret in a specific language or languages and signs the order allowing the interpreter to be considered for appointment on *Provisional Qualification of Noncertified or Nonregistered Spoken Language Interpreter* **(form INT-110).**

(B) A provisional qualification is valid for one year from the date of judicial officer signature on form INT-110.

(C) Interpreters seeking a third or subsequent provisional qualification period after January 1, 2025, must demonstrate their efforts to achieve certified or registered status, by providing the following information to the court, either orally or on form INT-110:

(i) Whether they have completed the Judicial Council's online self-paced court interpreter ethics training wihtin the past two years; and

(ii) Whether they have made at least two attempts to pass a qualifying exam in the past two years, if such a qualifying exam exists. Interpreters, including re- lay interpreters, working in a language for which an Oral Proficiency Exam exists must attempt that exam.

(D) When an interpreter seeks a third or subsequent provisional qualification period after January 1, 2025, the judicial officer must find that the interpreter has made the efforts required in (C) or must indicate that good cause exist to appoint the interpreter in form INT-110's *Provisional Qualification Finding and Order of the Court.*

(3) Required record

In addition to the matter that must be stated on the record uner (d)(2), to make a provisional appointment of a noncertified or nonregistered interpreter, the judicial officer in the proceeding mus state on the record:

(A) A finding that a certified or registered interpreter is not available and a statement that *Certification of Unavailability of Certified or Registered Interpreter and Availability of Provisionally Qualified Interpreter* **(form INT-120) for the language to be interpreted is on file for this date with the court administrator;**

(B) A finding that the interpreter has been provisionally qualified to interpret in the required language or languages, following procedures adopted by the Judicial Council (see forms INT-100-INFO and INT-25 110);

(C) A finding, if applicable, that there is a necessity to appoint the interpreter beyond the time ordinarily allowed in (4); and

(D) Whether a party has objected to the appointment of the proposed interpreter or has waived the appointment of a certified or registered interpreter.

(4) Limits on provisional appointment

(A) Unless the judicial officer in the proceeding determines there is a necessity, a noncertified interpreter who is provisionally qualified under this rule to interpret in Spanish may not interpret in a superior court for more than 45 court days or parts of court days within a calendar year.

(B) Unless the judicial officer in the proceeding determines there is a necessity, a noncertified or nonregistered in-

---

NOTE: Three asterisks (***) indicate unchanged material.

Rule 2.893   JANUARY 2025 SUPPLEMENT   4

terpreter who is provisionally qualified under this rule to interpret in a language other than Spanish may not interpret in a superior court for more than 75 court days or parts of court days within a calendar year.

(Subd (e) amended effective January 1, 2025.)

Rule 2.893 (e). 2024 Deletes. [1] Appointment of intermediary interpreters working between two languages that do not include English **[2]** An interpreter who works as an intermediary between two languages that do not include English (a relay interpreter) is not eligible to become certified or registered. However, a relay interpreter can become provisionally qualified if the judge finds that he or she is qualified to interpret the proceeding following procedures adopted by the Judicial Council (see forms INT-100-INFO, INT-110, and INT-120). The limitations in (f) below do not apply to relay interpreters.

[1] (f) Temporary appointment of noncertified or nonregistered interpreter&

(1) When permissible

If the judicial officer in a proceeding finds that a certified or registered interpreter is not available, a noncertified or nonregistered interpreter may be appointed to interpret for a single, brief, routine matter before the court in order to prevent burdensome delay or in other unusual circumstances.

(2) Required record

A noncertified or nonregistered interpreter may be appointed on a temporary basis, if, in addition to the requirements of (d)(2), the judicial officer in the proceeding finds on the record that:

(A) The LEP person has been informed of their right to an interpreter and has waived the appointment of a certified or registered interpreter or an interpreter who could be provisionally qualified by the judicial officer in the proceeding, as provided in (e);

(B) Good cause exists to appoint an interpreter who is not certified, registered, or provisionally qualified; and

(C) The interpreter is qualified to interpret that proceeding, following procedures adopted by the Judicial Council (see forms INT-100-INFO and INT-140).

(3) Limits on temporary appointment

The appointment of an interpreter under this subdivision is limited to a single, brief, routine matter before the court. The use of the interpreter in this circumstance may not be extended to subsequent proceedings without again following the procedure set forth in this subdivision.

(Sub (f) adopted effective January 1, 2025; previous subd (b) repealed effective January 1, 2025.)

Rule 2.893(f). 2024 Deletes. [1] Limit on appointment of provisionally qualified noncertified and nonregistered interpreters (1) A noncertified or nonregistered interpreter who is provisionally qualified under (d)(3) may not interpret in any trial court for more than any four six-month periods, except in the following circumstances: (A) A noncertified interpreter of Spanish may be allowed to interpret for no more than any two six-month periods in counties with a population greater than 80,000. (B) A noncertified or nonregistered interpreter may be allowed to interpret more than any four six-month periods, or any two six-month periods for an interpreter of Spanish under (f)(1)(A), if the judge in the proceeding makes a specific finding on the record in each case in which the interpreter is sworn that good cause exists to appoint the interpreter, notwithstanding the interpreter's failure to achieve Judicial Council certification. (2) Except as provided in (f)(3), each six-month period under (f)(1) begins on the date a presiding judge signs an order under (d)(3)(A)(ii) allowing the noncertified or nonregistered interpreter to be considered for appointment. (3) If an interpreter is provisionally qualified under (d)(3) in more than one court at the same time, each six-month period runs concurrently for purposes of determining the maximum periods allowed in this subdivision. (4) Beginning with the second six-month period under (f)(1), a noncertified or nonregistered interpreter may be appointed if he or she meets all of the following conditions: (A) The interpreter has taken the State of California Court Interpreter Written Exam at least once during the 12 calendar months before the appointment; (B) The interpreter has taken the State of California's court interpreter ethics course for interpreters seeking appointment as a noncertified or nonregistered interpreter, or is certified or registered

---

NOTE: Three asterisks (***) indicate unchanged material.

FOR UPDATES, CALL (800) 833-9844 Rule 2.893

in a different language from the one in which he or she is being appointed; and (C) The interpreter has taken the State of California's online court interpreter orientation course, or is certified or registered in a different language from the one in which he or she is being appointed. (5) Beginning with the third six-month period under (f)(1), a noncertified or nonregistered interpreter may be appointed if he or she meets all of the following conditions: (A) The interpreter has taken and passed the State of California Court Interpreter Written Exam with such timing that he or she is eligible to take a Bilingual Interpreting Exam; and (B) The interpreter has taken either the Bilingual Interpreting Exam or the relevant Oral Proficiency Exam(s) for his or her language pairing at least once during the 12 calendar months before the appointment.(6) The restrictions in (f)(5)(B) do not apply to any interpreter who seeks appointment in a language pairing for which no exam is available. (7) The restrictions in (f)(4) and (5) may be waived by the presiding judge for good cause whenever there are fewer than 25 certified or registered interpreters enrolled on the Judicial Council's statewide roster for the language requiring interpretation.

(g) Appointment of relay interpreter

(1) When permissible

If, after a diligent search, a certified or registered interpreter is not available to interpret between English and the language required for a court proceeding, the court may appoint a relay interpreter to interpret between two non-English spoken languages and a second interpreter who can interpret between one of the relay interpreter's languages and English. A relay interpreter may be appointed provisionally as described in (e), or on a temporary basis as described in (f).

(2) Required record

(A) If the relay interpreter is appointed as a provisional interpreter, the judicial officer must make the record required for all appointments of noncertified and nonregistered interpreters in (d)(2), must follow the rules for provisional qualification in (e)(2), and must make the record required in (e)(3).

(B) If the relay interpreter is appointed as a temporary interpreter, the judicial officer must make the record required for all appointments of noncertified and nonregistered interpreters in (d)(2) and the record required in (f)(2).

(3) Limits on appointment of relay interpreters

(A) A relay interpreter who is qualified for a provisional appointment described in (e) is subject to the time limits for appointment set forth in (e)(4).

(B) A relay interpreter with a temporary appointment described in (f) is subject to the limits on temporary appointment to a single, brief, and routine matter before the court.

(Sub (g) adopted effective January 1, 2025.)
Rule 2.893 amended effective January 1, 2025; adopted effective January 1, 2018.

Advisory Committee Comment

Subdivisions (c) and (d)(2). When a court reporter is transcribing the proceedings, or an electronic recording is being made of the proceedings, a [1] **judicial officer** may satisfy the "on the record" requirement by stating the required details of the interpreter appointment in open court. If there is no court reporter and no electronic recording is being made, the "on the record" requirement may be satisfied by stating the required details of the interpreter appointment and documenting them in writing—such as in a minute order, the official clerk's minutes, a formal order, or even a handwritten document—that is entered in the case file.

Subdivision [2] (f). This provision is intended to allow for the one-time use of a noncertified or nonregistered interpreter who is not provisionally qualified to interpret for an LEP person in a courtroom event. This provision is not intended to be used to meet the extended or ongoing interpretation needs of LEP court users.

[3] When determining whether the matter before the court is a "brief, routine matter" for which a noncertified or nonregistered interpreter who has not been provisionally qualified may be used, the judicial officer should consider the complexity of the matter at issue and likelihood of potential impacts on the LEP person's substantive rights, keeping in mind the consequences that could flow from inaccurate or incomplete interpretation of the proceedings.

Rule 2.893 Advisory Committee Comment. 2024 Deletes. [1] judge [2] (d)(4) [3] Subdivision (b)(7) and (d)(4)(f).

NOTE: Three asterisks (***) indicate unchanged material.

Title 3
Civil Rules

Division 11
Noticed Motions

Chapter 5
Noticed Motions

Rule 3.1308. Tentative rulings

(a) Tentative ruling procedures

A trial court that offers a tentative ruling procedure in civil law and motion matters must follow one of the following procedures:

(1) *Notice of intent to appear required*

The court must make its tentative ruling available by [1] **a** method designated by the court, by no later than 3:00 p.m. the court day before the scheduled hearing. If the court desires oral argument, the tentative ruling must so direct. The tentative ruling may also note any issues on which the court wishes the parties to provide further argument. If the court has not directed argument, oral argument must be permitted only if a party notifies all other parties and the court by 4:00 p.m. on the court day before the hearing of the party's intention to appear. A party must notify all other parties by telephone or in person. The court must accept notice by telephone and, at its discretion, may also designate alternative methods by which a party may notify the court of the party's intention to appear. The tentative ruling will become the ruling of the court if the court has not directed oral argument by its tentative ruling and notice of intent to appear has not been given.

(2) *No notice of intent to appear required*

The court must make its tentative ruling available by [2] **a** method designated by the court, by a specified time before the hearing. The tentative ruling may note any issues on which the court wishes the parties to provide further argument at the hearing. This procedure must not require the parties to give notice of intent to appear, and the tentative ruling will not automatically become the ruling of the court if such notice is not given. The tentative ruling, or such other ruling as the court may render, will not become the final ruling of the court until the hearing.

(Subd (a) amended effective January 1, 2025; previously amended effective July 1, 2000, and January 1, 2007.)

Rule 3.1308 (a).   2024 Deletes. [1] telephone and also, at the option of the court, by any other **[2]** telephone and also, at the option of the court, by any other

(b) No other procedures permitted

Other than following one of the tentative ruling procedures authorized in (a), courts must not issue tentative rulings except:

(1) By posting a calendar note containing tentative rulings on the day of the hearing; or

(2) By announcing the tentative ruling at the time of oral argument.

(c) Notice of procedure

A court that follows one of the procedures described in (a) must so state in its local rules. The local rule must specify the [1] **method** for obtaining the tentative rulings and the time by which the rulings will be available.

(Subd (c) amended effective January 1, 2025; previously amended effective July 1, 2000, and January 1, 2007.)

Rule 3.1308 (c).   2024 Deletes. [1] telephone number

(d) Uniform procedure within court or branch

If a court or a branch of a court adopts a tentative ruling procedure, that procedure must be used by all judges in the court or branch who issue tentative rulings.

(e) Tentative rulings not required

This rule does not require any judge to issue tentative rulings.

Rule 3.1308 amended effective January 1, 2025; adopted as rule 324 effective July 1, 1992; previously amended effective July 1, 2000; previously amended and renumbered effective January 1, 2007.

NOTE: Three asterisks (***) indicate unchanged material.

Division 12
Settlement

Rule 3.1385. Duty to notify court and others of settlement of entire case

(a) Notice of settlement

(1) *Court and other persons to be notified*

If an entire case is settled or otherwise disposed of, each plaintiff or other party seeking affirmative relief must immediately file written notice of the settlement or other disposition with the court and serve the notice on all parties and any arbitrator or other court-connected alternative dispute resolution (ADR) neutral involved in the case. Each plaintiff or other party seeking affirmative relief must also immediately give oral notice to all of the above if a hearing, conference, or trial is scheduled to take place within 10 days.

(2) *Compensation for failure to provide notice*

If the plaintiff or other party seeking affirmative relief does not notify an arbitrator or other court-connected ADR neutral involved in the case of a settlement at least 2 days before the scheduled hearing or session with that arbitrator or neutral, the court may order the party to compensate the arbitrator or other neutral for the scheduled hearing time. The amount of compensation ordered by the court must not exceed the maximum amount of compensation the arbitrator would be entitled to receive for service as an arbitrator under Code of Civil Procedure section 1141.18(b) or that the neutral would have been entitled to receive for service as a neutral at the scheduled hearing or session.

(b) Dismissal of case

Except as provided in (c) or (d), each plaintiff or other party seeking affirmative relief must serve and file a request for dismissal of the entire case within 45 days after the date of settlement of the case. If the plaintiff or other party required to serve and file the request for dismissal does not do so, the court must dismiss the entire case 45 days after it receives notice of settlement unless good cause is shown why the case should not be dismissed.

(c) Conditional settlement

(1) *Notice*

If the settlement agreement conditions dismissal of the entire case on the satisfactory completion of specified terms that are not to be performed within 45 days of the settlement, including payment in installment payments, the notice of conditional settlement served and filed by each plaintiff or other party seeking affirmative relief must specify the date by which the dismissal is to be filed.

(2) *Dismissal*

If the plaintiff or other party required to serve and file a request for dismissal within 45 days after the dismissal date specified in the notice does not do so, the court must dismiss the entire case unless good cause is shown why the case should not be dismissed.

(3) *Hearings vacated*

(A) Except as provided in (B), on the filing of the notice of conditional settlement, the court must vacate all hearings and other proceedings requiring the appearance of a party and may not set any hearing or other proceeding requiring the appearance of a party earlier than 45 days after the dismissal date specified in the notice, unless requested by a party.

(B) The court need not vacate a hearing on an order to show cause or other proceeding relating to sanctions, or for determination of good faith settlement at the request of a party under Code of Civil Procedure section 877.6.

(4) *Case disposition time*

Under standard 2.2(n)(1)(A), the filing of a notice of conditional settlement removes the case from the computation of time used to determine case disposition time.

(d)–(e) * * *

Advisory Committee Comment

Subdivisions (a) and (b). Amended Code of Civil Procedure section 664.6 allows parties to settle a case and agree to have the case dismissed without prejudice. The plaintiff or other party seeking affirmative relief must follow the procedures outlined in subdivisions (a) and (b) even if the parties settle the case and agree to dismiss under the provisions of Code of Civil Procedure section 664.6.

Subdivision (c). Code of Civil Procedure section 664.6 allows for but does not mandate

---

NOTE: Three asterisks (***) indicate unchanged material.

the dismissal of cases with conditional settlements either upon stipulation of the parties or on the court's own motion. Subdivision (c) provides an alternative process for cases with a conditional settlement in which dismissal is not sought under Code of Civil Procedure section 664.6.

Division 19
Proceedings

Rule 3.1905. Debtor's examinations in consumer debt cases

(a) Service of order to appear for examination

A judgment creditor who serves *Application and Order to Appear for Examination—Consumer Debt* (form EJ-141) or *Application and Order to Produce Financial Statement or Appear for Examination—Consumer Debt* (form SC-136), as provided in Code of Civil Procedure section 708.111(c), must include copies of *Information on Debtor's Examinations Regarding Consumer Debt* (form EJ-140-INFO/SC-136-INFO) and *Current Dollar Amounts of Exemptions From Enforcement of Judgments* (form EJ-156) with the service.

(b) Filing of notice of motion and motion to require examination

A judgment creditor who files *Notice of Motion and Motion to Require Examination—Consumer Debt* (form EJ-146) to move the court to require the judgment debtor to appear for examination, as provided in Code of Civil Procedure section 708.111(d), must physically or electronically attach a copy of the judgment debtor's *Financial Statement—Consumer Debt* (form EJ-144) to the motion.

Rule 3.1905 adopted effective January 1, 2025.

Advisory Committee Comment

The requirements of subdivision (a) are in addition to those of Code of Civil Procedure section 708.111(c), including that a judgment creditor who serves form EJ-141 on a judgment debtor must include blank copies of *Notice of Financial Statement—Consumer Debt* (form EJ5143), *Financial Statement—Consumer Debt* (form EJ-144), and *Exemptions From the Enforcement of Judgments (form EJ-155) with the service.*

Division 22
Petitions Under the California Environmental Quality Act

Chapter 2
California Environmental Quality Act Proceedings Involving Streamlined CEQA Projects

Article 1
General Provisions

Rule 3.2226. Application

(a) Timing of conference

The court [1] **must** hold an initial case management conference within 30 days of the filing of the petition or complaint.

(Sub (a) amended effective January 1, 2025.)

Rule 3.2226(a). 2024 Deletes. [1] should

(b) Notice

Petitioner must provide notice of the case management conference to respondent, real party in interest, and any responsible agency or party to the action who has been served before the case management conference, within one court day of receiving notice from the court or at time of service of the petition or complaint, whichever is later.

(c) Subjects for consideration

At the conference, the court should consider the following subjects:

(1) Whether all parties named in the petition or complaint have been served;

(2) Whether a list of responsible agencies has been provided, and notice provided to each;

(3) Whether all responsive pleadings have been filed, and if not, when they must be filed, and whether any hearing is required to address them;

(4) Whether severance, bifurcation, or consolidation with other actions is desirable, and if so, a relevant briefing schedule;

NOTE: Three asterisks (***) indicate unchanged material.

FOR UPDATES, CALL (800) 833-9844 Rule 3.2226

(5) Whether to appoint a liaison or lead counsel, and either a briefing schedule on this issue or the actual appointment of counsel;

(6) **The scope, timing, and cost of the record of proceedings, including** whether the [2] record has been certified and served on all parties, whether there are any issues with it, and whether the court wants to receive a paper copy;

(7) Whether the parties anticipate any motions before the hearing on the merits concerning discovery, injunctions, or other matters, and if so, a briefing schedule for these motions;

(8) What issues the parties intend to raise in their briefs on the merits, and whether any limitation of issues to be briefed and argued is appropriate;

(9) Whether a schedule for briefs on the merits different from the schedule provided in these rules is appropriate;

(10) Whether the submission of joint briefs on the merits is appropriate, and the page limitations on all briefs, whether aggregate per side or per brief;

(11) When the hearing on the merits of the petition will be held, and the amount of time appropriate for it;

(12) The potential for settlement, and whether a schedule for settlement conferences or alternative dispute resolution should be set;

(13) Any stipulations between the parties;

(14) Whether a further case management conference should be set; and

(15) Any other matters that the court finds appropriate.

(Sub (c) amended effective January 1, 2025.)

Rule 3.2226(c). 2024 Deletes. [1] administrative **[2]**

(d) Joint case management conference statements

At least three court days before the case management conference, petitioner and all parties that have been served with the petition must serve and file a joint case management conference statement that addresses the issues identified in (c) and any other pertinent issues.

(e) Preparation for the conference

At the conference, lead counsel for each party and each self-represented party must appear in person or remotely, must be familiar with the case, and must be prepared to discuss and commit to the party's position on the issues listed in (c).

Rule 3.2226 amended effective January 1, 2025; adopted July 1, 2014; previously amended effective January 21, 2022.

NOTE: Three asterisks (***) indicate unchanged material.

TITLE 4
Criminal Rules

Division 5
Felony Sentencing Law

Rule 4.433. Matters to be considered at time set for sentencing

(a)–(b) * * *

(c) If a sentence of imprisonment is to be imposed, or if the execution of a sentence of imprisonment is to be suspended during a period of probation, the sentencing judge must:

(1) Determine, under section 1170(b), whether to impose one of the three authorized terms of imprisonment referred to in section 1170(b), or any enhancement, and state on the record the reasons for imposing that term;

(2) Determine whether any additional term of imprisonment provided for an enhancement charged and found will be stricken;

(3) Determine whether the sentences will be consecutive or concurrent if the defendant has been convicted of multiple crimes;

(4) Determine any issues raised by statutory prohibitions on the dual use of facts and statutory limitations on enhancements, as required in rules 4.420(c) and 4.447; and

(5) Pronounce the court's judgment and sentence, stating the terms thereof and giving reasons for those matters for which reasons are required by law.

(d) * * *

(e) When a sentence of imprisonment is imposed under (c) or under rule 4.435, the sentencing judge must inform the defendant:

(1) **Of** the parole period provided by section 3000 **under section 1170(c), or the parole period provided by section 3000.01,** to be served after expiration of the sentence, in addition to any period of incarceration for parole violation;

(2) Of the period of postrelease community supervision provided by section 3456 to be served after expiration of the sentence, in addition to any period of incarceration for a violation of postrelease community supervision; or

(3) Of any period of mandatory supervision imposed under section 1170(h)(5)(A) and (B), in addition to any period imprisonment for a violation of mandatory supervision.

(Subd (e) amended effective January 1, 2025; previously amended effective July 28, 1977, January 1, 1979, July 1, 2003, January 1, 2007, January 1, 2017, and January 1, 2018.)

Rule 4.433(e). 2024 Deletes. [1] Under section 1170(e)

Rule 4.433 amended effective January 1, 2025; adopted as rule 433 effective July 1, 1977; previously renumbered effective January 1, 2001; previously amended effective July 28, 1977, January 1, 1979, July 1, 2003, January 1, 2007, May 23, 2007, January 1, 2008, January 1, 2017, and January 1, 2018.

Advisory Committee Comment

This rule summarizes the questions that the court is required to consider at the time of sentencing, in their logical order.

Subdivision (a)(2) makes it clear that probation should be considered in every case, without the necessity of any application, unless the defendant is statutorily ineligible for probation.

Under subdivision (b), when imposition of sentence is to be suspended, the sentencing judge is not to make any determinations as to possible length of a term of imprisonment on violation of probation (section 1170(b)). If there was a trial, however, the judge must state on the record the circumstances that would justify imposition of one of the three authorized terms of imprisonment based on the trial evidence.

Subdivision (d) makes it clear that all sentencing matters should be disposed of at a single hearing unless strong reasons exist for a continuance.

NOTE: Three asterisks (***) indicate unchanged material.

Title 5
Family and Juvenile Rules

Division 1
Family Rules

Chapter 6
Request for Court Orders

Article 2
Filing and Service

Rule 5.92. Request for court order; responsive declaration

(a) Application

(1) In a family law proceeding under the Family Code:

(A) The term "request for order" has the same meaning as the terms "motion" or "notice of motion" when they are used in the Code of Civil Procedure;

(B) A *Request for Order* (form FL-300) must be used to ask for court orders, unless another Judicial Council form has been adopted or approved for the specific request; and

(C) A *Responsive Declaration to Request for Order* (form FL-320) must be used to respond to the orders sought in form FL-300, unless another Judicial Council form has been adopted or approved for the specific purpose.

(2) In an action under the Domestic Violence Prevention Act [1]:

(A) While the restraining order in a *Restraining Order After Hearing (Order of Protection)* (form DV-130) is still in effect, *Request to Change or End Restraining Order* (form DV-300) must be used to ask that the court modify or terminate the orders granted in form DV-130, including any orders for child custody, child support, spousal or domestic partner support, property, or other orders.

(B) After the restraining order in a *Restraining Order After Hearing* (Order of Protection) (form DV-130) expires, *Request for Order* (form FL-300) must be used to ask that the court modify or terminate any orders in form DV-130 that remain in effect, such as child custody, child support, spousal or domestic partner support, property, or other orders.

(C) To respond to the request described in:

(i) Subdivision (a)(2)(A), *Response to Request to Change or End 22 Restraining Order* (form DV-320) must be used.

(ii) Subdivision (a)(2)(B), *Response to Request for Order* (form 25 FL-320) must be used.

(3) In a case initiated in the juvenile dependency court, if the court granted *Juvenile Restraining Order After Hearing* (form JV-255), the juvenile case has been closed (dismissed), and the restraining order is still in effect:

(A) *Request to Change or End Restraining Order* (form DV-300) must be used to ask that the court modify or terminate the order if it was granted under the Domestic Violence Prevention Act.

(B) *Request for Order* (form FL-300) must be used to ask that the court modify or terminate the order if it was granted under the Code of Civil Procedure.

(C) To respond to the request described in:

(i) Subdivision (a)(3)(A), *Response to Request to Change or End Restraining Order* (form DV-320) must be used.

(ii) Subdivision (a)(3)(B), *Response to Request for Order* (form 2 FL-320) must be used.

(4) * * *

(Subd (a) amended effective January 1, 2025; adopted effective July 1, 2016; previous subd (a) repealed effective July 1, 2016.)

Rule 5.92(a). 2024 Deletes. [1] , a Request for Order (form FL-300) must be used to request a modification or termination of all orders made after a hearing on Restraining Order After Hearing (form DV-130).

(b) Request for order; required forms and filing procedure

(1) The *Request for Order* (form FL-300) must set forth facts sufficient to notify

---

NOTE: Three asterisks (***) indicate unchanged material.

the other party of the moving party's contentions in support of the relief requested.

(2) Except in actions under Family Code section 6344, in which a party seeks an order for attorney's fees and costs, when a party seeks orders for spousal or domestic partner support, attorney's fees and costs, or other orders relating to the parties' property or finances:

(A) The party must complete an *Income and Expense Declaration* (form FL-150) and file it with the *Request for Order* (form FL-300); and

(B) * * *

(c)–(g) * * *

Advisory Committee Comment

The Family and Juvenile Law Advisory Committee and the Elkins Implementation Task Force developed rule 5.92 and *Request for Order* (form FL-300) in response to *Elkins Family Law Task Force: Final Report and Recommendations (April 2010)* for one comprehensive form and related procedures to replace the *Order to Show Cause* (form FL-300) and *Notice of Motion* (form FL-301). (See page 35 of the final report online at *www.courts.ca.gov/elkins-finalreport.pdf.*)

NOTE: Three asterisks (***) indicate unchanged material.

TITLE 5
Family and Juvenile Rules

Division 3
Juvenile Rules

Chapter 8
Restraining Orders, Custody Orders, and Guardianships General Court Authority

Rule 5.620. Orders after filing under section 300

(a) * * *

(b) Restraining orders (§ 213.5)

After a petition has been filed under section 300, and until the petition is dismissed or dependency is terminated, the court may issue restraining orders as provided in rule 5.630. A temporary restraining order must be prepared on [1] *Temporary Restraining Order—Juvenile* (form JV-250). An order after hearing must be prepared on *Juvenile Restraining Order After Hearing* (form JV-255).

(Subd (b) amended effective January 1, 2025; previously amended effective January 1, 2007, January 1, 2014, and January 1, 2023.)

Rule 5.620(b). 2024 Deletes. [1] *Notice of Court Hearing and*

(c)–(e) * * *

Rule 5.620 amended effective January 1, 2025; adopted as rule 1429.1 effective January 1, 2000; previously amended and renumbered as rule 5.620 effective January 1, 2007; previously amended effective January 1, 2014, January 1, 2016, January 1, 2021, and January 1, 2023.

Rule 5.625. Orders after filing of petition under section 601 or 602

(a) Restraining orders (§ 213.5)

After a petition has been filed under section 601 or 602, and until the petition is dismissed or wardship is terminated, the court may issue restraining orders as provided in rule 5.630. A temporary restraining order must be prepared on [1] *Temporary Restraining Order—Juvenile* (form JV-250) or, if the restrained person is the

subject of a petition under section 601 or 602, on [2] *Temporary Restraining Order Against a Child* (form JV-260). An order after hearing must be prepared on *Juvenile Restraining Order After Hearing* (form JV-255) or, if the restrained person is the subject of a petition under section 601 or 602, on [3] **Juvenile Restraining Order Against a Child—Order After Hearing (form JV-265).**

(Subd (a) amended effective January 1, 2025; previously amended effective January 1, 2003, and January 1, 2007, January 1, 2014, and January 1, 2023.)

Rule 5.625(a). 2024 Deletes. [1] *Notice of Court Hearing and* [2] *Notice of Court Hearing and* [3] *Juvenile Restraining Order After Hearing—Against a Child*

(b)–(c) * * *

Rule 5.625 amended effective January 1, 2025; adopted as rule 1429.3 effective January 1, 2000; previously amended effective January 1, 2003, January 1, 2014, January 1, 2021, and January 1, 2023; previously amended and renumbered effective January 1, 2007.

Rule 5.630. Restraining orders

(a)–(b) * * *

(c) Application for restraining orders

(1)–(7) * * *

(8) The temporary restraining order must be prepared on *Temporary Restraining Order—Juvenile* (form JV-250) or, if the restrained person is the subject of a petition under section 601 or 602, on *Temporary Restraining Order Against a Child* (form JV-260), and must state on its face the date of expiration of the order.

(Subd (c) amended January 1, 2025; adopted as subd (b); previously amended effective January 1, 2003, January 1, 2004, January 1, 2007, and January 1, 2012; amended and relettered effective January 1, 2023.)

Rule 5.630(c). 2024 Deletes. [1] *Notice of Court Hearing and* [2] *Notice of Court Hearing and*

(d) Continuance

(1)–(3) * * *

(4) Either *Order on Request to Reschedule Restraining Order Hearing* (form JV-253) or a new *Notice of Court Hearing* [1]

NOTE: Three asterisks (***) indicate unchanged material.

(form JV-249) may be used to grant or deny a request for a continuance and, if granted, a *Temporary Restraining Order— Juvenile* (form JV-250) [2] **may be issued.** If the restrained person is the subject of a petition under section 601 or 602, either form JV-253 or a new *Notice of Court Hearing* [3] **(form JV-249) may be used and, if granted,** *Temporary Restraining Order Against a Child* (form JV-260) [4] **may be issued**.

(Subd (d) amended January 1, 2025; adopted as subd (g) effective January 1, 2003; amended and relettered as subd (e) effective January 1, 2012 and as subd (d) effective January 1, 2023; previously amended effective January 1, 2004, January 1, 2007, January 1, 2014, and July 1, 2016.)

Rule 5.630(d). 2024 Deletes. [1] and **[2]** must be used to grant or deny a request for continuance **[3]** and **[4]** must be used

[1] (e) Hearing on application for restraining order

(1)–(4) * * *

(Subd (e) relettered effective January 1, 2025; adopted as subd (d); previously amended effective January 1, 2007, and January 1, 2014; previously amended and relettered as subd (h) effective January 1, 2003, and as subd (f) effective January 1, 2012; as subd (e) effective January 1, 2023.)

Rule 5.630(e). 2024 Deletes. [1] (f)

(f) Service of [1] firearms prohibition forms

When service of [2] *Temporary Restraining Order—Juvenile* (form JV-250) [3], *Temporary Restraining Order Against a Child* (form JV-260), *Juvenile Restraining Order After Hearing* (form JV-255) [4], or *Juvenile Restraining Order Against a Child—Prder After Hearing* (form JV-265) is made, it must be served with a blank *Receipt for Firearms, Firearm Parts, and Ammunition* (form DV-800/JV-270) and *How Do I Turn In, Sell, or Store Firearms, Firearm Parts, and Ammunition?* (form DV-800-INFO/JV-270-INFO). Failure to serve form JV-270 or JV-270-INFO does not make service of form JV-250, form JV-255, form JV-260, or form JV-265 invalid.

(Subd (f) amended effective January 1, 2025; adopted as subd (g) effective January 1, 2012; previously amended effective January 1, 2014, and July 1, 2014; previously amended and relettered effective January 1, 2023.)

Rule 5.630(f). 2024 Deletes. [1] restraining order **[2]** *Notice of Court Hearing and* **[3]** *Notice of Court Hearing and* **[4]** *Juvenile Restraining Order After Hearing— Against a Child*

(g)–(i) * * *

(j) Modification of restraining order

(1) When a juvenile court case is open a restraining order may be terminated or modified as follows:

[1] **(A)** A restraining order may be **terminated or** modified on the court's own motion or in the manner provided for in section 388 or 778, as appropriate, and rule 5.570.

[2] **(B)** A termination or modification order must be made on [3] ***Order to Change or End Restraining Order After Hearing*** **(form JV-257).**

[4] **(C)** A **modification order must also be made on a** new *Restraining Order After Hearing* (form JV-255) or, if the restrained person is the subject of a petition under section 601 or 602, a new [5] ***Juvenile Restraining Order Against a Child— Order After a Hearing*** **(form JV-265). [6]**

(2) When a juvenile court case is closed ***Restraining Order After Hearing*** **(form JV-255) may be terminated or modified under rule 5.92.**

(Subd (j) amended effective January 1, 2025; adopted as subd (j) effective January 1, 2012; previously amended effective January 1, 2014; previously relettered as subd (k) effective July 1, 2014; previously amended and relettered as subd (j) effective January 1, 2023.)

Rule 5.630(j). 2024 Deletes. [1] (1) **[2]** (2) **[3]** *Change to Restraining Order After Hearing* **[4]** (3) **[5]** *Juvenile Restraining Order After Hearing—Against a Child* **[6]** , may be prepared in addition to form JV-257.

Rule 5.630 amended effective January 1, 2025; adopted as rule 1429.5 effective January 1, 2000; amended and renumbered effective January 1, 2007; previously amended effective January 1, 2003, January 1, 2004, January 1, 2012, January 1, 2014, July 1, 2014, July 1, 2016, and January 1, 2023.

Rule 5.632. Civil harassment, workplace violence prevention, and domestic violence prevention orders

A proceeding for the following orders initiated by or brought against a child who

---

NOTE: Three asterisks (***) indicate unchanged material.

FOR UPDATES, CALL (800) 833-9844   Rule 5.676

has previously been adjudged a dependent child or a ward of the juvenile court and who remains under juvenile court jurisdiction must be heard in the juvenile court that has jurisdiction of the child as required by Code of Civil Procedure section 374.5:

(1) An order prohibiting harassment under Code of Civil Procedure section 527.6;

(2) An order prohibiting violence in the workplace under Code of Civil Procedure section 527.8;

(3) A protective order under division 10 (beginning with section 6200) of the Family Code; and

(4) A protective order under Family Code sections 7710 and 7720.

Rule 5.632 adopted effective January 1, 2025.

Chapter 12
Cases Petitioned Under Section 300

Article 1
Initial Hearing

Rule 5.674. Conduct of hearing; admission, no contest, submission

(a) * * *

(b) Detention hearing; general conduct (§ 319; 42 U.S.C. § 600 et seq.)

(1) The court must read, consider, and reference **the social worker's report as described in section 319(b),** any **other report** [1] submitted by the social worker, and any relevant evidence submitted by any party or counsel. All detention findings and orders must appear in the written orders of the court.

(2) * * *

(Subd (b) amended effective January 1, 2025; adopted effective July 1, 2002; previously amended effective January 1, 2007, January 1, 2016, and January 1, 2020.)

Rule 5.674(b). 2024 Deletes. [1] reports

(c)–(e) * * *

Rule 5.674 amended effective January 1, 2025; repealed and adopted as rule 1444 effective January 1, 1998; previously amended and renumbered as rule 5.674 effective January 1, 2007; previously amended effective July 1, 2002, January 1, 2016, January 1, 2017, and January 1, 2020.

Rule 5.676. Requirements for detention

(a) Requirements for detention (§ 319)

No child may be ordered detained by the court unless the court finds that:

(1) A prima facie showing has been made that the child is described by section 300;

(2) Continuance in the home of the parent, Indian custodian, or guardian is contrary to the child's welfare; and

(3) One or more of the grounds for detention in [1] section 319(c)(1)(A)–(D) is [2] present.

(Subd (a) amended effective January 1, 2025; previously amended effective July 1, 2002, 23 January 1, 2007, and January 1, 2020.)

Rule 5.676(a). 2024 Deletes. [1] rule 5.678 [2] found

(b) * * *

(c) Evidence required at detention hearing

In making the findings required to support an order of detention, the court may rely solely on written police reports, probation or social worker reports, or other documents.

The reports relied on must include **the required information in section 319(b) and:**

[1] **(1)** A description of the services that have been provided, including those under section 306, and of any available services or safety plans that would prevent or eliminate the need for the child to remain in custody;

[2] **(2)** If a parent is enrolled in a certified substance abuse treatment facility that allows a dependent child to reside with **the** parent, information and a recommendation regarding whether the child can be returned to the custody of that parent; [3]

[4] **(3)** If continued detention is recommended, information about any parent or guardian of the child with whom the child was not residing at the time the child was taken into custody and about any relative or nonrelative extended family member as defined under section 362.7 with whom the child may be detained.

(Subd (c) amended effective January 1, 2025; adopted as subd (b); previously amended effective July 1, 2002, and January 1, 2007; previously relettered effective January 1, 2020.)

NOTE: Three asterisks (***) indicate unchanged material.

Rule 5.678   JANUARY 2025 SUPPLEMENT   16

Rule 5.676(c).   2024 Deletes. [1] (1) A statement of the reasons the child was removed from the parent's custody; (2) **[2]** (3) **[3]** his or her **[4]** (4) Identification of the need, if any, for the child to remain in custody; **[5]** (5)

(d) Additional evidence required at detention hearing for Indian child

If it is known, or there is reason to know the child is an Indian child, the reports relied on must also include:

(1) A statement of the risk of imminent physical damage or harm to the Indian child and any evidence that the emergency removal or placement continues to be necessary to prevent the imminent physical damage or harm to the child;

(2) The steps taken to provide notice to the child's parents, Indian custodian, and tribe about the hearing under section 224.3;

(3) If the child's parents and Indian custodian are unknown, a detailed explanation of what efforts have been made to locate and contact them, including contact with the appropriate Bureau of Indian Affairs regional director;

(4) The residence and the domicile of the Indian child;

(5) If either the residence or the domicile of the Indian child is believed to be on a reservation or in an Alaska Native village, the name of the tribe affiliated with that reservation or village;

(6) The tribal affiliation of the child and of the parents or Indian custodian;

(7) A specific and detailed account of the circumstances that caused the Indian child to be taken into temporary custody;

(8) If the child is believed to reside or be domiciled on a reservation in which the tribe exercises exclusive jurisdiction over child custody matters, a statement of efforts that have been made and that are being made to contact the tribe and transfer the child to the tribe's jurisdiction; [1]

(9) A statement of the efforts that have been taken to assist the parents or Indian custodian so the Indian child may safely be returned to their custody [2]; **and**

(10) The steps taken to consult and collaborate with the tribe and the outcome of that consultation and collaboration.

(Subd (d) amended effective January 1, 2025; adopted effective January 1, 2020.)

Rule 5.676(d).   2024 Deletes. [1] and **[2]** ;

Rule 5.676 amended effective January 1, 2025; repealed and adopted as rule 1445 effective January 1, 1998; previously amended effective July 1, 2002, January 1, 2016, and January 1, 2020; previously amended and renumbered as rule 5.676 effective January 1, 2007.

Rule 5.678.   Findings in support of detention; factors to consider; reasonable efforts; active efforts; detention alternatives

(a) Findings in support of detention (§ 319; 42 U.S.C. § 672)

The court must order the child released from custody unless the court makes findings as specified in section 319(c)(**1**), and where it is known, or there is reason to know the child is an Indian child, the additional finding specified in section 319(d).

(b)–(c) * * *

(d) Orders of the court (§ 319; 42 U.S.C. § 672)

(1) If the court orders the child detained, the court must, in a written order or on the record, order that temporary care and custody of the child be vested with the county welfare department pending disposition or further order of the court and must make the other findings and orders specified in section 319(c)(2), (e), and (f)(3).

(2) When making the determination in section 319(c)(2)(B)(ii) that the placement complies with less disruptive alternatives, the court must also consider whether measures are available to alleviate disruption to the child and minimize the impact of removal and whether those measures have been utilized. In addition to considering the factors listed in section 319(c)(2)(A)(i) to (iv) related to the impact of removal and less disruptive alternatives, the court may consider factors that include, but are not limited to whether the current placement:

(A) Can accommodate the proposed visitation schedule.

(B) Will disrupt the child's extracurricular activities or other services, including but not limited to medical, dental, mental health, and educational services.

(C) Will allow the child to observe their religious or cultural practices

(D) Can accommodate the child's special needs.

NOTE: Three asterisks (***) indicate unchanged material.

(e) * * *

Rule 5.678 amended effective January 1, 2025; repealed and adopted as rule 1446 effective January 1, 1998; previously amended and re-numbered as rule 5.678 effective January 1, 2007; previously amended effective January 1, 1999, July 1, 2002, January 1, 2016; and January 1, 2019.

NOTE: Three asterisks (***) indicate unchanged material.

Title 7
Probate and Mental Health Rules

Division 1
Probate Rules

Chapter 21
Guardianships

Rule 7.1016. Participation and testimony of wards in guardianship proceedings (Prob. Code, § 1514(b)(1); Fam. Code, § 3042)

(a) Definitions

As used in this rule [1]:

(1) "Ward" includes **a** [2] proposed ward. [3]

[4] (2) "Party," [5] **when referring** to [6] a ward, [7] **indicates** a ward who has filed a petition or [8] **made a response or objection** to a petition [9] **in a probate guardianship proceeding.**

(Subd (a) amended effective January 1, 2025.)

Rule 7.1016(a). 2024 Deletes. [1] , the following terms have the meanings specified **[2]** " **[3]** " **[4]** A "proceeding" is a matter before the court for decision in a probate guardianship of the person that concerns appointment or removal of a guardian, visitation, determination of the ward's place of residence, or termination of the guardianship by court order. **[5]** as used in this rule to **[6]** the **[7]** means **[8]** opposition **[9]** concerning a proceeding or other matter subject to this rule

(b) Purpose and scope [1]

(1) This rule applies [2] to the participation and testimony [3] a ward in a [4] **hearing on:**

(A) Appointment or removal of a **guardian** of the person, **including appointment of a successor guardian;**

(B) Parental visitation of a ward in a guardianship of the person; or

(C) Termination of a guardianship of the person. [5]

(2) The court **may,** in its discretion, [6] apply **all or part** of this rule [7] to the participation and testimony of a ward **in a hearing** in a guardianship of the estate or [8] **a hearing in a guardianship of the person on a matter not described in (1).**

(3) [9] **This rule does not require a ward to address the** court or prohibit [10] **a ward** from doing so. [11]

(4) [12] Rule 5.250 [13] **does not apply to** probate guardianship proceedings.

(5) Nothing in this rule limits the application of Evidence Code sections 765(b) and 767(b) to the testimony of a minor in a guardianship proceeding.

(Subd (b) amended effective January 1, 2025.)

Rule 7.1016(b). 2024 Deletes. [1] of rule **[2]** Family Code section 3042 **[3]** the **[4]** proceeding in a probate **[5]** The testimony of other minors in a guardianship case is governed by Evidence Code sections 765(b) and 767(b). **[6]** may, **[7]** , in whole or in part, **[8]** in a matter before the court in a guardianship of the person that is not a proceeding within the meaning of this rule. The phrase "or other matter subject to this rule" following the term "proceeding" is a reference to the matters described in this paragraph **[9]** No statutory mandate, rule, or practice requires a ward who is not a party to the proceeding or other matter subject to this rule to participate in **[10]** prohibits him or her **[11]** When a ward desires to participate but is not a party to the proceeding or other matter subject to this rule, the court must balance the protection of the ward, the statutory duty to consider the wishes of and other input from the ward, and the probative value of the ward's input while ensuring all parties' due process rights to challenge evidence relied on by the court in making decisions affecting the ward in matters covered by the rule. **[12]** This rule rather than rule **[13]** , on children's participation and testimony in family court proceedings, applies in

(c) Determining whether [1] a ward wishes to address the court or has changed their preference about addressing the court

(1) The following persons must inform the [2] **judicial officer** if they [3] **are aware** that a ward [4] wishes to address the court [5]:

(A) The ward's [6] **attorney or guardian ad litem;**

(B) A court or county guardianship investigator;

(C) A child custody recommending counselor who provides recommendations to the judicial officer under Family Code section 3183; **or**

NOTE: Three asterisks (***) indicate unchanged material.

FOR UPDATES, CALL (800) 833-9844 Rule 7.1016

(D) An expert appointed by the court under Evidence Code section 730 to assist the court in the matter. [7][8]

(2) [9] **A party to the proceeding or party's attorney** may inform the [10] **judicial officer** [11] that a ward [12] wishes to address the [13] court. [14]

(3) In the absence of information indicating that a ward [15] wishes to address the court, [16] the judicial officer may inquire whether the ward wishes to do so.

(4) If a ward informs any of the persons specified in (1) that the ward has changed their preference about addressing the court, that person must, as soon as feasible, inform the parties or their attorneys, the ward's attorney or guardian ad litem, the court investigator, and the judicial officer of that change.

(Subd (c) amended effective January 1, 2025.)

Rule 7.1016(c). 2024 Deletes. [1] the nonparty **[2]** court **[3]** have information indicating **[4]** who is not a party **[5]** in a proceeding or other matter subject to this rule **[6]** counsel; **[7]** ; or. **[8]** (E) The ward's guardian ad litem. **[9]** The following persons **[10]** court **[11]** if they have information indicating who is not a party **[12]** court in a proceeding or other matter subject to this rule: **[13]** (A) A party in the guardianship case; and (B) An attorney for a party in the guardianship case. **[14]** who is not a party **[16]** , in a proceeding or other matter subject to this rule,

(d) [1] Determining whether addressing the court is in [2] a ward's best interest

(1) [3] **If** a ward [4] wishes to address the court, the judicial officer must consider whether [5] **permitting** the ward [6] **to address the court** is in the ward's best interest.

(2) If the ward is 12 years old or older, the judicial officer must [7] **permit** the ward **to address the court** unless the court [8] **finds** that addressing the court is not in the ward's best interest and states the reasons **for that finding** on the record.

(3) If the ward is younger than 12 years of age, the court may permit the ward to address the court if the court finds that addressing the court is appropriate and in the ward's best interest.

(4) In determining whether addressing the court is in the ward's best interest, the

judicial officer should consider the following:

(A) Whether the ward is of sufficient age and capacity to form an intelligent preference as to the matter to be decided;

(B) Whether the ward is of sufficient age and capacity to understand the nature of testimony;

(C) Whether [9] the ward may be at risk **of emotional [10] emotioanlly [11] harm if permitted or denied the opportunity to address the court; [12]**

(D) Whether the ward may benefit from addressing the court;

[13] **(E)** Whether the **subjects** [14] about which the ward is anticipated to address the court are relevant to the **court's** decision [15];

[16] **(F)** Whether [17] appointment of [18] **an attorney** or a guardian ad litem for the ward would be helpful to the determination or [19] necessary to protect the ward's interests; and

[20] **(G)** Whether any other factors weigh in favor of or against [21] **permitting** the ward **to** address the court, taking into consideration the ward's desire to do so.

(Subd (d) amended effective January 1, 2025.)

Rule 7.1016(d). 2024 Deletes. [1] Guidelines for determining **[2]** the nonparty **[3]** When **[4]** who is not a party indicates that he or she**[5]** involving **[6]** in the proceeding or other matters subject to this rule **[7]** hear from **[8]** makes a finding **[9]** information has been presented indicating that **[10]** emtionally **[11]** he or she is **[12]** or that **[13]** (D) **[14]** subject areas **[15]** the court must make **[16]** (E) **[17]** the **[18]** counsel under Probate Code section 1470 **[19]** would be **[20]** (F) **[21]** having

(e) [1] Receiving testimony and other input from [2] a ward [3]

(1) Unless the court determines that permitting a ward to address the court in the presence of the parties would be in the ward's best interest and states the reasons for that finding on the record, the court must not permit the ward to address the court in the presence of the parties.

(2) In determining the best interest of the ward under (1), the court must consider whether addressing the court in the presence of the parties is likely to be detrimental to the ward.

NOTE: Three asterisks (***) indicate unchanged material.

Rule 7.1016   JANUARY 2025 SUPPLEMENT   20

(3) If the court does not permit the ward to address the court in the presence of the parties, the court must provide an alternative method for the ward to address the court so that the court can obtain input directly from the ward on the record. If a court reporter is not available, the court must provide other means to obtain the ward's input and make it available to the parties and their attorneys.

[4] **(4)** In taking testimony from a ward, [5] the court must [6] **exercise** the special care required by Evidence Code [7] **sections** 765(b) **and 767(b) to the extent that those sections apply. In addition, [8] if** the ward is not represented by an attorney **and the court does not appoint one,** the court must inform the ward in an age-appropriate manner about the [9] **limits on the** confidentiality of testimony and that the information provided to the court will be on the record and provided to the parties in the case.

[10] **(5)** In [11] listening to and inviting the ward's input, the court must allow but not require the ward to state a preference regarding the matter to be decided [12] and should provide information in an age-appropriate manner about the process by which the court will make a decision.

[13] (6) In any case in which a ward [14] will [15] testify, the court must consider [16] **appointing an attorney or a guardian ad litem** for the ward. [17] **The ward's attorney or guardian ad litem** must:

(A) Provide information to the ward in an age-appropriate manner about the [19] [18] **limits** on the confidentiality of testimony and indicate to the ward [20] that **the** information provided to the court will be on the record and provided to the parties in the case;

(B) [21] **Provide** information to the ward in an age-appropriate manner about the process by which the court will make a decision;

(C) If appropriate, provide the ward with an orientation to the courtroom or other place where the ward will testify; and

(D) Inform the parties and the court about the ward's desire to **testify or otherwise** provide input.

[22] **(7)** If the court precludes [23] a ward **from testifying** as a witness [24], **the court must provide** alternatives **to testimony** [25] for [26] **obtaining information about the ward's preferences** or other input [27]. **These alternatives** may include:

(A) [28] **Participate of a** court or county guardianship investigator [29] in the case under Probate Code section 1513 or 1513.2;

(B) Appointment of a child custody evaluator or investigator under Evidence Code section 730;

(C) Appointment of [30] **an attorney** or a guardian ad litem for the ward;

(D) [31] **Recipet of admissible** evidence provided by the ward's parents, parties, or witness in the proceeding or other matter subject to this rule;

(E) [32] **Receipt of information from** a child custody recommending counselor authorized under Family Code section 3183 to make a recommendation to the court; and

(F) [33] **Receipt of information** from a child interview center or professional to avoid unnecessary multiple interviews.

[34] **(8)** If the court precludes [35] a ward [36] **from testifying** as a witness [37] and specifies an alternative [38] **to testimony,** the court must require that the information [39] obtained [40] **through that** alternative [41] and provided by a professional (other than [42] **an attorney** for the ward or [43] for [44] party) or [45] **other** nonparty:

(A) Be **documented** in writing and fully [46] **reflect the views expressed by** the [47] **ward's** on the matters [48] **to be decided**;

(B) Describe the ward's input in sufficient detail to assist the court in making its decision;

(C) Be **obtained and** provided to the court and to the parties by a person who will be available for testimony and cross-examination; and

(D) Be filed in the confidential portion of the case file.

(Subd (e) amended effective January 1, 2025.)

Rule 7.1016(e). 2024 Deletes. [1] Guidelines for receiving **[2]** the nonparty **[3]** (1) No testimony of a ward may be received without such testimony being heard on the record or in the presence of the parties. This requirement

---

NOTE: Three asterisks (***) indicate unchanged material.

21 FOR UPDATES, CALL (800) 833-9844 Rule 7.1016

may not be waived. (2) On deciding to take the testimony of a ward who is not a party in a proceeding or other matter subject to this rule, the judicial officer should balance the necessity of taking the ward's testimony in the courtroom with parents, the guardian or proposed guardian, other parties, and attorneys present with the need to create an environment in which the ward can be open and honest. In each case in which a ward's testimony will be taken, the judicial officer should consider: (A) Where the testimony will be taken; (B) Who should be present when the testimony is taken; (C) How the ward will be questioned; and (D) Whether a court reporter is available in all instances, but especially when the ward's testimony may be taken outside the presence of the parties and their attorneys. If the court reporter will not be available, whether there are other means to collect, preserve, transcribe, and make the ward's testimony available to parties and their attorneys. [4] (3) [5] , who is not a party to the proceeding or other matter subject to this rule, [6] take [7] If [8] limitations [9] (4) [10] the process of [11] in the proceeding or other matter subject to this rule [12] (5) [13] who is not a party to the proceeding or other matter subject to this rule [14] be called to [15] the appointment of counsel for the ward under Probate Code section 1470 and may consider the appointment of a guardian ad litem [16] In addition to satisfying the requirements for minor's counsel under rule 7.1101, minor's counsel [17] limitations [18] the possibility [19] Allow but not require the ward to state a preference regarding the issues to be decided in the proceeding or other matter subject to this rule, and provide [20] testify or otherwise [21] (6) [22] the calling of [23] who is not a party [24] in a proceeding or other matter subject to this rule [25] the court to [26] from the ward [27] A [28] participating [29] counsel [30] Admissible [31] Information provided by [32] Information provided [33] (7) [34] the calling of [35] who is not a party [36] in a proceeding or other matter subect to this rule [37] one of the other [38] alternatives [39] or evidence [40] by [41] means [42] counsel [43] counsel [44] any [45] a [46] document [47] ward's views [48] on which he or she wished to express an opinion

(f) Responsibilities of court-connected or appointed professionals [1]

A child custody evaluator, an expert witness appointed under Evidence Code section 730, an investigator, **or** a child custody recommending counselor [2] **who is** appointed or assigned to [3] **obtain information from** a ward **and provide the information to the court and the parties** must:

(1) [4] **Inform** the ward in an age-appropriate manner about the [5] **limits** on **the** confidentiality of testimony and [6] that information provided to the professional [7] **will** be shared with the court on the record and provided to the parties in the case;

(2) [8] **and Inform the ward** in an age-appropriate manner about the process by which the court will make a decision; [9]

(3) Allow but not require the ward to state a preference regarding the issues to be decided by the court; and

[10] (4) [11] **Give** the other parties [12] information about how best to support [13] the ward during the court process.

(Subd (f) amended effective January 1, 2025.)

Rule 7.1016(f). 2024 Deletes. [1] – all wards **[2]** or other custody mediator **[3]** meet with **[4]** Provide information to **[5]** limitations **[6]** the possibility **[6]** may **[7]** Allow but not require the ward to state a preference regarding the issues to be decided in the proceeding or other matter subject to this rule, **[8]** provide information **[9]** and **[10]** (3) **[11]** Provide to **[12]** in the case **[13]** the interest of

(g) [1] Providing [2] information and support [3]

Courts should provide information to [4] parties and **information and support** to [5] **a** ward [6] **if** the ward wants to participate or testify. Methods of providing information **or support** may include:

(1) [7] **Directing** court or county guardianship investigators [8] **or** experts appointed under Evidence Code section 730 **to** meet jointly or separately with the parties and their attorneys to discuss alternatives to having the ward provide direct testimony;

(2) Providing an orientation for the ward [9] **to** the court process and the role of the judicial officer in making decisions, [10] the **setup of the** courtroom or chambers [11] **where the ward will testify or address the court,** and [12] **the process of** participating or testifying [13];

(3) Providing information to parties before the ward participates or testifies so that they can consider the possible effect **of participating or testifying** on the ward [14];

(4) Appointing [15] **an attorney** or a guardian ad litem for the ward to assist in

---

NOTE: Three asterisks (***) indicate unchanged material.

Rule 7.1016 JANUARY 2025 SUPPLEMENT 22

the provision of information to the ward concerning his or her decision to participate [16] or testify;

(5) Including information in guardianship orientation presentations and publications about the options available to a ward [17] to participate or testify or not to do so, and the consequences of a ward's decision [18] to become a party to the proceeding [19]; and

(6) Providing an interpreter for the ward.

(Subd (g) amended effective January 1, 2025.)

Rule 7.1016(g).   2024 Deletes. [1] Methods of providing **[2]** to parties **[3]** supporting nonparty wards **[4]** the **[5]** the **[6]** who is not a party to the proceeding or other matter subject to this rule when if **[7]** Having **[8]** and **[9]** about **[10]** how **[11]** will be set up **[12]** what **[13]** will entail; **[14]** not participating in the proceeding or other matter subject to this rule; **[15]** counsel under Probate Code section 1470 **[16]** in the proceeding **[17]** who is not a party to the proceeding or other matter subject to this rule **[18]** whether **[19]** or other matter subject to this rule

(h) If [1] a ward is a party [2]

(1) A ward who is a party [3] is subject to the law of discovery [4] **applicable** to parties in civil actions and may be called as a witness by any other party unless the court makes a finding that [5] **requiring the ward to respond** to discovery requests or **testify** [6] as a witness [7] **would** not **be** in the ward's best interest and states the reasons **for that finding** on the record.

(2) The court must consider appointing [8] **an attorney** or a guardian ad litem for a ward who is a party [9] if the ward is not represented [10].

(3) In determining whether [11] **requiring a ward to respond to** discovery requests or [12] **testifying** as a witness [13] **would be** in the ward's best interest, the judicial officer should consider [14]:

(A) Whether [15] the ward may be at risk **of** [16] **emotional harm** if [17] **required to respond** to discovery requests or [18] **testify;**

(B) Whether the [19] **subjects that** the **ward's responses or testimony** [20] are expected to address are relevant to the **court's** decision; [21] and

(C) Whether any other factors weigh in favor of or against [22] **requiring** the ward

[23] **to respond** discovery requests or **testify.**

(4) In taking testimony from a ward [24], the court must [25] **exercise** the special care required by Evidence Code [26] **sections** 765(b) **and 767(b) to the extent that those sections apply. In addition, if** [27] the ward is not represented by an attorney **and the court does not appoint one**, the court must inform the ward in an age-appropriate manner about the [28] **limits** on **the** confidentiality of testimony and that the information provided to the court will be on the record and provided to the parties in the case.

(Subd (h) amended effective January 1, 2025.)

Rule 7.1016(h).   2024 Deletes. [1] the **[2]** to the proceeding **[3]** to the proceeding or other matter subject to this rule **[4]** applied **[5]** providing information in response **[6]** testifying **[7]** is **[8]** counsel under Probate Code section 1470 an attorney **[9]** to the proceeding or other matter subject to this rule **[10]** by counsel **[11]** providing information in response **[12]** testifying **[13]** is **[14]** the following **[15]** information has been presented indicating that **[16]** emotionally **[17]** he or she is permitted or denied the opportunity to provide information in response **[18]** by testimony **[19]** subjects areas about which **[20]** is anticipated to provide information in response to discovery requests or by testimony **[21]** the court must make **[22]** having **[23]** provide information in response **[24]** by testimony **[25]** who is a party to the proceeding or other matter subject to this rule, **[26]** take **[27]** If **[28]** limitations

(i) Education and training [1]

Education and training [2] for court staff and judicial officers should include information on:

(1) A [3] **ward's** participation in [4] **guardianship hearings;**

(2) Methods other than direct testimony for [5] a ward **to give relevant information and input to the court;** [6]

(3) Procedures [7] for taking a ward's testimony [8] **consistent with the safeguards in this rule, Family Code section 3042, and Evidence Code sections 765(b) and 767(b);** and

(4) The differences in the application of this rule to wards who are **parties** and **those who** are not [10].

(Subd (i) amended effective January 1, 2025.)

NOTE: Three asterisks (***) indicate unchanged material.

Rule 7.1016(i). 2024 Deletes. [1] of judicial officers and court staff [2] content [3] wards' [4] proceedings or other matters subject to this rule, [5] receiving input from [6] , [7] procedures [8] , [9] parties to the proceeding or other matters subject to this rule.

Rule 7.1016 adopted effective January 1, 2013.

NOTE: Three asterisks (***) indicate unchanged material.

Title 8
Appellate Rules

Division 1
Rules Relating to the Supreme Court and COurts of Appeal

Chapter 2
Civil Appeals

Article 1
Taking the Appeal

Rule 8.100.   Filing the appeal

(a)–(f) * * *

(g) Civil case information statement

(1) Within 15 days after **the reviewing court [1] assigns the appeal a case number,** the appellant must serve and file in the reviewing court a completed *Civil Case Information Statement* (form APP-004), attaching a copy of the judgment or appealed order that shows the date it was entered.

(2) * * *

(Subd (g) amended effective January 1, 2025; adopted as subd (f) effective January 1, 2003; previously amended and relettered as subd (g) effective January 1, 2008; previously amended effective January 1, 2007, January 1, 2014, and January 1, 2016.)

Rule 8.100(g).   2024 Deletes. [1] superior court clerk sends the notification of the filing of the notice of appeal required by (e)(1)

Rule 8.100 amended effective January 1, 2025; repealed and adopted as rule 1 effective January 1, 2002; previously amended and renumbered as rule 8.100 effective January 1, 2007; previously amended effective January 1, 2003, August 17, 2003, January 1, 2008, July 1, 2009, July 27, 2012, January 1, 2014, January 1, 2016, and January 1, 2018.

Advisory Committee Comment

Subdivision (a). In subdivision (a)(1), the reference to "judgment" is intended to include part of a judgment. Subdivision (a)(1) includes an explicit reference to "appealable order" to ensure that litigants do not overlook the applicability of this rule to such orders.

Subdivision (c)(2). This subdivision ad-

dresses the content of a clerk's notice that a check for the filing fee has been dishonored or that the reviewing court has received a notice of appeal without the filing fee, a certificate of cash payment, or an application for, or order granting, a fee waiver. Rule 8.26(f) addresses what an appellant must do when a fee waiver application is denied.

Subdivision (e). Under subdivision (e)(2), a notification of the filing of a notice of appeal must show the date that the clerk sent the document. This provision is intended to establish the date when the 20-day extension of the time to file a cross-appeal under rule 8.108(e) begins to run.

Subdivision (e)(1) requires the clerk to send a notification of the filing of the notice of appeal to the appellant's attorney or to the appellant if unrepresented. Knowledge of the date of that notification allows the appellant's attorney or the appellant to track the running of the 20-day extension of time to file a cross-appeal under rule 8.108(e).

Article 3
Briefs in the Court of Appeals

Rule 8.200.   Briefs by parties and amici curiae

(a)–(b) * * *

(c) Amicus curiae briefs

(1) Within 14 days after the last appellant's reply brief is filed or could have been filed under rule 8.212, whichever is earlier, any person or entity may serve and file an application for permission of the presiding justice to file an amicus curiae brief. **If no respondent's brief is filed, the application is due within days after the respondent's brief could have been filed.** For good cause, the presiding justice may allow later filing.

(2)–(6) * * *

(7) The Attorney General may file an amicus curiae brief without the presiding justice's permission, unless the brief is submitted on behalf of another state officer or agency. The Attorney General must serve and file the brief within 14 days after the last appellant's reply brief is filed or could have been filed under rule 8.212, which-

---

NOTE: Three asterisks (***) indicate unchanged material.

ever is earlier [1]. **If no respondent's brief is filed, the Attorney General must serve and file the amicus curiae brief within 34 days after the respondent's brief could have been filed. The brief** must provide the information required by (2) and comply with (5). Any party may serve and file an answer within 14 days after the brief is filed.

(Subd (c) amended effective January 1, 2025; adopted as subd (b); previously relettered effective January 1, 2003; previously amended effective January 1, 2007, January 1, 2008, and January 1, 2009.)

Rule 8.200(c).   2024 Deletes. [1] , and *Rule 8.200 amended effective January 1, 2025; repealed and adopted as rule 13 effective January 1, 2002; previously amended and renumbered effective January 1, 2007; previously amended effective January 1, 2003, January 1, 2008, January 1, 2009, and January 1, 2017.*

Advisory Committee Comment

Subdivision (a)(2). * * *

Subdivision (b). * * *

Subdivision (c)(1). The time within which a reply brief "could have been filed under rule 8.212" includes any authorized extension of the deadline specified in rule 8.212. **The time within which a respondent's brief "could have been filed" includes any authorized extension of the deadline specified in rule 8.212 and the 15-day default notice period specified in rule 8.220(a).**

Chapter 3
Criminal Appeals

Article 3
Record on Appeal

Rule 8.320.   Normal record; exhibits

(a) Contents

If the defendant appeals from a judgment of conviction, or if the People appeal from an order granting a new trial, the record must contain a clerk's transcript and a reporter's transcript, which together constitute the normal record.

(b) Clerk's transcript

The clerk's transcript must contain:

(1) The accusatory pleading and any amendment;

(2) Any demurrer or other plea;

(3) All court minutes;

(4) All jury instructions that any party submitted in writing and the cover page required by rule 2.1055(b)(2) indicating the party requesting each instruction, and any written jury instructions given by the court;

(5) Any written communication between the court and the jury or any individual juror;

(6) Any verdict;

(7) Any written opinion of the court;

(8) The judgment or order appealed from and any abstract of judgment or commitment;

(9) Any motion for new trial, with supporting and opposing memoranda and attachments;

(10) The notice of appeal and any certificate of probable cause filed under rule 8.304(b);

(11) Any transcript of a sound or sound-and-video recording furnished to the jury or tendered to the court under rule 2.1040;

(12) Any application for additional record and any order on the application;

(13) And, if the appellant is the defendant:

(A) Any written defense motion denied in whole or in part, with supporting and opposing memoranda and attachments;

(B) If related to a motion under (A), any search warrant and return and the reporter's transcript of any preliminary examination or grand jury hearing;

(C) Any document admitted in evidence to prove a prior juvenile adjudication, criminal conviction, or prison term;

(D) The probation officer's report; and

(E) Any court-ordered diagnostic or psychological report required under Penal Code section 1203.03(b) or 1369.

(c) Reporter's transcript

The reporter's transcript must contain:

(1) The oral proceedings on the entry of any plea other than a not guilty plea;

(2) The oral proceedings on any motion in limine;

(3) The oral proceedings at trial, but excluding the voir dire examination of jurors and any opening statement;

(4) All instructions given orally;

(5) Any oral communication between the court and the jury or any individual juror;

NOTE: Three asterisks (***) indicate unchanged material.

Rule 8.320

(6) Any oral opinion of the court;

(7) The oral proceedings on any motion for new trial;

(8) The oral proceedings at sentencing, granting or denying of probation, or other dispositional hearing;

(9) And, if the appellant is the defendant:

(A) The oral proceedings on any defense motion denied in whole or in part except motions for disqualification of a judge and motions under Penal Code section 995;

(B) The closing arguments; and

(C) Any comment on the evidence by the court to the jury.

(d) Limited normal record in certain appeals

If the People appeal from a judgment on a demurrer to the accusatory pleading, or if the defendant or the People appeal from an appealable order other than a ruling on a motion for new trial, the normal record is composed of:

(1) *Clerk's transcript*

A clerk's transcript containing:

(A) The accusatory pleading and any amendment;

(B) Any demurrer or other plea;

(C) Any written motion or notice of motion granted or denied by the order appealed from, with supporting and opposing memoranda and attachments;

(D) The judgment or order appealed from and any abstract of judgment or commitment;

(E) Any court minutes relating to the judgment or order appealed from and:

(i) If there was a trial in the case, any court minutes of proceedings at the time the original verdict is rendered and any subsequent proceedings; or

(ii) If the original judgment of conviction is based on a guilty plea or nolo contendere plea, any court minutes of the proceedings at the time of entry of such plea and any subsequent proceedings;

(F) The notice of appeal; and

(G) If the appellant is the defendant, all probation officer reports and any court-ordered diagnostic report required under Penal Code section 1203.03(b).

(2) *Reporter's transcript*

(A) A reporter's transcript of any oral proceedings incident to the judgment or order being appealed; and

(B) If the appeal is from an order after judgment, a reporter's transcript of:

(i) The original sentencing proceeding; and

(ii) If the original judgment of conviction is based on a guilty plea or nolo contendere plea, the proceedings at the time of entry of such plea.

(e) Exhibits

Exhibits admitted in evidence, refused, or lodged are deemed part of the record, but may be transmitted to the reviewing court only as provided in **(g)(2) or** rule 8.224.

(Subd (e) amended effective January 1, 2025; previously amended effective January 1, 24 2007.)

(f) Stipulation for partial transcript

If counsel for the defendant and the People stipulate in writing before the record is certified that any part of the record is not required for proper determination of the appeal, that part must not be prepared or sent to the reviewing court.

(g) Additional clerk's transcript materials required by local rule

In addition to the items listed in (b) and (d)(1), the reviewing court may, by local rule, require the clerk's transcript to include any or all additional court records contained in the superior court file.

(1) For purposes of this provision, "court records" has the meaning provided in rule 2.502(3).

(2) The reviewing court's local rule may require the clerk's transcript to include copies of exhibits admitted into evidence, refused, or lodged.

(Subd (g) adopted effective January 1, 2025.)
Rule 8.320 amended effective January 1, 2025; repealed and adopted as rule 31 effective January 1, 2004; previously amended and renumbered effective January 1, 2007; previously amended effective January 1, 2005, January 1, 2008, January 1, 2010, January 1, 2013, and January 1, 2014.

Advisory Committee Comment

Rules 8.45–8.46 address the appropriate handling of sealed and confidential records that must be included in the record on appeal. Examples of confidential records include Penal Code section 1203.03 diagnostic reports, records closed to inspection by court order under *People v. Marsden*

NOTE: Three asterisks (***) indicate unchanged material.

(1970) 2 Cal.3d 118 or *Pitchess v. Superior Court* (1974) 11 Cal.3d 531, in-camera proceedings on a confidential informant, and defense expert funding requests (Pen. Code, § 987.9; *Keenan v. Superior Court* (1982) 31 Cal.3d 424, 430).

Subdivision (d)(1)(E). This rule identifies the minutes that must be included in the record. The trial court clerk may include additional minutes beyond those identified in this rule if that would be more cost-effective.

Subdivision (g). This rule authorizes the Courts of Appeal to adopt local rules that require additional court records, as defined by rule 2.502(3), to be included in the clerk's transcript, up to all court records in the superior court file. For purposes of this rule, items excluded from the definition of "court records" under rule 2.502(3) are not considered part of the superior court file.

Rule 8.483 governs the normal record and exhibits in civil commitment appeals.

Division 4
Rules Relating to the Supreme Court Appellate Division

Chapter 4
Brieds, Hearing, and Decision in Limited Civil and Misdemeanor Appeals

Rule 8.883.   Contents and form of briefs

(a) * * *

(b) Length

(1) **Except as providedin (4),** a brief produced on a computer must not exceed 6,800 words, including footnotes. Such a brief must include a certificate by appellate counsel or an unrepresented party stating the number of words in the brief. The person certifying may rely on the word count of the computer program used to prepare the brief.

(2) A brief produced on a typewriter must not exceed 20 pages.

(3) The information listed on the cover, any table of contents or table of authorities, the certificate under (1), and any signature block are excluded from the limits stated in (1) or (2).

(4) If a party uses a form brief approved for use by the Judicial Council, the brief, including any attachments, may not exceed 25 pages in length. Attachments must comply with the formatting requirements stated in (c)(1) through (c)(7).

(5) On application, the presiding judge may permit a longer brief for good cause. A lengthy record or numerous or complex issues on appeal will ordinarily constitute good cause. If the court grants an application to file a longer brief, it may order that the brief include a table of contents and a table of authorities.

(Subd (b) amended effective January 1, 2025; previously amended effective January 1, 2011, and January 1, 2013.)

(c) Form

(1) A brief may be reproduced by any process that produces a clear, black image of letter quality. All documents filed must have a page size of 8½ by 11 inches. If filed in paper form, the paper must be white or unbleached and of at least 20-pound weight. Both sides of the paper may be used if the brief is not bound at the top.

(2) Any conventional font may be used. The font may be either proportionally spaced or monospaced.

(3) The font style must be roman; but for emphasis, italics or boldface may be used or the text may be underscored. Case names must be italicized or underscored. Headings may be in uppercase letters.

(4) Except as provided in (11), the font size, including footnotes, must not be smaller than 13-point.

(5) The lines of text must be at least one-and-a-half-spaced. Headings and footnotes may be single-spaced. Quotations may be block-indented and single-spaced. Single-spaced means six lines to a vertical inch.

(6) The margins must be at least 1½ inches on the left and right and 1 inch on the top and bottom.

(7) The pages must be consecutively numbered.

(8) The cover—or first page if there is no cover—must include the information required by rule 8.816(a)(1).

NOTE: Three asterisks (***) indicate unchanged material.

Rule 8.883 — JANUARY 2025 SUPPLEMENT — 28

(9) If filed in paper form, the brief must be bound on the left margin, except that briefs may be bound at the top if required by a local rule of the appellate division. If the brief is stapled, the bound edge and staples must be covered with tape.

(10) The brief need not be signed.

(11) If the brief is produced on a typewriter:

(A) A typewritten original and carbon copies may be filed only with the presiding judge's permission, which will ordinarily be given only to unrepresented parties proceeding in forma pauperis. All other typewritten briefs must be filed as photocopies.

(B) Both sides of the paper may be used if a photocopy is filed; only one side may be used if a typewritten original and carbon copies are filed.

(C) The type size, including footnotes, must not be smaller than standard pica, 10 characters per inch. Unrepresented incarcerated litigants may use elite type, 12 characters per inch, if they lack access to a typewriter with larger characters.

(d) * * *

Advisory Committee Comment

Subdivision (b). Subdivision (b)(1) states the maximum permissible lengths of briefs produced on a computer in terms of word count rather than page count. This provision tracks a provision in rule 8.204(c) governing Court of Appeal briefs and is explained in the comment to that provision. Subdivision (b)(3) specifies certain items that are not counted toward the maximum brief length. Signature blocks, as referenced in this provision, include not only the signatures, but also the printed names, titles, and affiliations of any attorneys filing or joining in the brief, which may accompany the signature.

Subdivision (b)(4) provides the maximum length of a brief, with attachments, if the party uses a form brief approved for use by the Judicial Council. The Judicial Council has approved the following optional form briefs that parties may use in limited civil appeals where there is no cross-appeal: *Appellant's Opening Brief—Limited Civil Case* **(form APP-200),** *Respondent's Brief—Limited Civil Case* **(form APP-201), and** *Appellant's Reply Brief—Limited Civil Case* **(form APP-202).**

NOTE: Three asterisks (***) indicate unchanged material.

Title 10
Judicial Administration Rules

Division 2
Administration of the Judicial Branch

Chapter 7
Minimum Education Requirements, Expectations, and Recommendation

Rule 10.461. Minimum education requirements for Supreme Court and Court of Appeal justices

(a) Applicability

All California Court of Appeal justices must complete the minimum judicial education requirements for new justices under (b), and all Supreme Court and Court of Appeal justices must complete minimum continuing education requirements as outlined under (c). All justices **must complete education requirements on fairness and access as stated in rule 10.465(a) and** should participate in more judicial education than is required, related to each individual's responsibilities and in accordance with the judicial education recommendations [1] **stated in rule 10.469.**

(Subd (a) amended effective January 1, 2025; adopted effective January 1, 2008.)

Rule 10.461(a). 2024 Deletes. [1] set forth

(b)–(e) * * *

Rule 10.461 amended effective January 1, 2025; adopted effective January 1, 2007; previously amended effective January 1, 2008, August 15, 2008, January 1, 2012, January 1, 2013, January 1, 2016, and January 1, 2023

Advisory Committee Comment

The requirements formerly contained in subdivision (e)(2) of rule 970, which has been repealed, are carried forward without change in rule 10.461(b).

Judicial Council staff have developed an individual reporting form that justices may use in tracking their own participation in education as required by rule 10.461(e)(1). The form is available from the council's Center for Judicial Education and Research. The Chief Justice and the administrative presiding justices may determine which form should be used in their court and may provide the council-developed form or another appropriate form developed by their court or by another court.

Rule 10.462. Minimum education requirements and expectations for trial court judges and subordinate judicial officers

(a) Applicability

All California trial court judges must complete the minimum judicial education requirements for new judges under (c)(1) and are expected to participate in continuing education as outlined under (d). All subordinate judicial officers must complete the minimum education requirements for new subordinate judicial officers under (c)(1) and for continuing education as outlined under (d). **All trial court judges and subordinate judicial officers must complete education requirements on fairness and access as stated in rule 10.465(a).** All trial court judges and subordinate judicial officers who hear family law matters must complete additional education requirements [1] **as stated** in rule 10.463. All trial court judges and subordinate judicial officers who hear [2] matters **specified in rule 10.464(a)** must participate in education on domestic violence issues as provided in rule 10.464. All trial court judges and subordinate judicial officers regularly assigned to hear probate proceedings must complete additional education requirements [3] **as stated** in rule 10.468. All trial court judges and subordinate judicial officers should participate in more judicial education than is required and expected, related to each individual's responsibilities and particular judicial assignment or assignments and in accordance with the judicial education recommendations as [4] **stated** in rule 10.469.

(Subd (a) amended effective January 1, 2025; previously amended effective January 1, 2008, and January 1, 2012.)

Rule 10.462 (a). 2024 Deletes. [1] set forth [2] certain types [3] set forth [4] set forth

---

NOTE: Three asterisks (***) indicate unchanged material.

(b)–(g) * * *

Rule 10.462 amended effective January 1, 2025; adopted effective January 1, 2007; previously amended effective January 1, 2008, July 1, 2008, August 15, 2008, January 1, 2012, January 1, 2013, January 1, 2016, and January 1, 2023

Advisory Committee Comment

The minimum judicial education requirements in rule 10.462 do not apply to retired judges seeking to sit on regular court assignment in the Temporary Assigned Judges Program. Retired judges who seek to serve in the Temporary Assigned Judges Program must comply with the education requirements included in the program's standards and guidelines established by the Chief Justice.

Judicial Council staff have developed an individual reporting form that judges may use in tracking their own participation in education as required by rule 10.462(f). The form is available from the council's Center for Judicial Education and Research. Presiding judges may determine which form should be used in their court and may provide the council-developed form or another appropriate form developed by their court or by another court.

Rule 10.465. Education requirements and recommendations for justices, judges, and subordinate judicial officers on fairness and access

(a) Education on bias and the prevention of harassment, discrimination, retaliation, and inappropriate workplace conduct

(1) Each justice, judge, and subordinate judicial officer must participate in bias education (including explicit, implicit, and/or unconscious bias).

(2) Each justice, judge, and subordinate judicial officer must participate in education on the prevention of harassment, discrimination, retaliation, and inappropriate workplace conduct.

(3) The education in (1) and (2) must be taken at least once every three-year continuing education cycle as determined under rules 10.461(c)(1) and 10.462(d).

(b) Additional education on fairness and access

To achieve the objective of assisting judicial officers in preserving the integrity and impartiality of the judicial system through the prevention of bias, each justice, judge, and subordinate judicial officer should regularly participate in education on fairness and access in addition to that required in (a). The education should include the following subjects: race and ethnicity, gender, sexual orientation, and persons with disabilities, persons with limited economic means, and persons without stable housing.

Rule 10.465 adopted effective January 1, 2025.

Rule 10.469. Education recommendations for justices, judges, and subordinate judicial officers

(a)–(d) * * *

[1]

Rule 10.469(e). 2024 Deletes. [1] (e) Education on fairness and access, unconscious bias, and prevention of harassment, discrimination, retaliation, and inappropriate workplace conduct (1) In order to achieve the objective of assisting judicial officers in preserving the integrity and impartiality of the judicial system through the prevention of bias, each justice, judge, and subordinate judicial officer should regularly participate in education on fairness and access. The education should include the following subjects: race and ethnicity; gender; sexual orientation; persons with disabilities; persons with limited economic means; and persons without stable housing. (2) Each justice, judge, and subordinate judicial officer must participate in education on unconscious bias, as well as the prevention of harassment, discrimination, retaliation, and inappropriate workplace conduct. This education must be taken at least once every three-year continuing education cycle as determined by rules 10.461(c)(1) and 10.462(d).

Rule 10.469 amended effective January 1, 2025; adopted effective January 1, 2008; previously amended effective January 1, 1999, January 1, 2012, January 1, 2015, January 1, 2016; January 1, 2021, and January 1, 2023; previously amended and renumbered effective January 1, 2007.

NOTE: Three asterisks (***) indicate unchanged material.

Standards of Judicial Administration

Title 10
Standards for Judicial Administration

Standard 2.2. Trial court case disposition time goals

(a)–(*l*) * * *

(m) Cases removed from court's control excluded from computation of time

If a case is removed from the court's control, the period of time until the case is restored to court control should be excluded from the case disposition time goals. The matters that remove a case from the court's control for the purposes of this section include:

(1) * * *

(2) Felony or misdemeanor cases:

(A) * * *

(C) Pendency of completion of **any** diversion **program** under **part 2 of title 6 of the** Penal Code **(commencing with** section 1000) [1];

(D)–(J) * * *

(Subd (m) amended effective January 1, 2025; adopted as subd (n) effective January 1, 2004; previously amended effective January 1, 2007); previously relettered and amended effective January 1, 2024.)

Standard 2.2. 2024 Deletes. [1] et seq.

(n) * * *

Standard 2.2 amended effective January 1, 2025; adopted as sec. 2.1 effective July 1, 1987; previously amended effective January 1, 1988, July 1, 1988, January 1, 1989, January 1, 1990, July 1, 1991, January 1, 2004, and January 1, 2024; previously amended and renumbered effective January 1, 2007.

NOTE: Three asterisks (***) indicate unchanged material.

SUPPLEMENT INDEX

A

APPELLATE RULES, SUPREME COURT AND COURTS OF APPEAL
Chief Justice
  Education of judicial branch
    Bias, fairness and access, and the prevention of inappropriate workplace conduct CRC 10.465
Justices
  Education of judicial branch
    Bias, fairness and access, and the prevention of inappropriate workplace conduct CRC 10.465

C

CONTINUING EDUCATION
Judges
  Bias, fairness and access, and the prevention of inappropriate workplace conduct CRC 10.465
Justices
  Bias, fairness and access, and the prevention of inappropriate workplace conduct CRC 10.465

COURTS OF APPEAL
Education of judicial branch
  Justices
    Bias, fairness and access, and the prevention of inappropriate workplace conduct CRC 10.465
Justices
  Education of judicial branch
    Bias, fairness and access, and the prevention of inappropriate workplace conduct CRC 10.465

D

DEFINITIONS
Relay interpreter
  Interpreters, appointment in court proceedings CRC 2.893

DOMESTIC VIOLENCE
Emergency protective orders CRC 5.632
Orders CRC 5.632
Temporary restraining order CRC 5.632
  Harassment generally, temporary restraining order and injunction prohibiting CRC 5.632

E

EMPLOYER AND EMPLOYEE
Injunctive relief action by employer for threats of violence towards employees CRC 5.632
Temporary restraining order to prevent violence toward employee, employer's action for CRC 5.632

ENFORCEMENT OF JUDGMENTS
Consumer debt
  Debtor's examination CRC 3.1905
  Exemption of principal residence from execution of judgment lien CCP §699.730
Examination proceedings
  Consumer debt
    Awards on or after January 1, 2025 CCP §708.111
    Debtor's examination CRC 3.1905

H

HARASSMENT
Injunctive relief CRC 5.632
Protective orders CRC 5.632

I

INJUNCTIONS
Employer's action for injunctive relief against threats of violence towards employees CRC 5.632
Harassment
  Prevention CRC 5.632
Temporary restraining orders
  Employer's action against threats of violence towards employee CRC 5.632
  Workplace violence, employer's action against CRC 5.632
Workplace violence, employer's action to prevent CRC 5.632

J

JUDGES
Subordinate judicial officers
  Education of judicial branch employees
    Bias, fairness and access, and the prevention of inappropriate workplace conduct CRC 10.465
Trial court, judicial branch education
  Subordinate judicial officers
    Bias, fairness and access, and the prevention of inappropriate workplace conduct CRC 10.465

JUDICIAL ADMINISTRATION RULES
Education of judicial officers
  Bias, fairness and access, and the prevention of inappropriate workplace conduct CRC 10.465
  Fairness and access education
    Bias, fairness and access, and the prevention of inappropriate workplace conduct CRC 10.465

P

PROTECTIVE ORDERS
Emergency protective orders CRC 5.632
Harassment CRC 5.632

I-1

PROTECTIVE ORDERS—Cont.
Workplace violence or threats of violence, injunctions or orders against
Firearm possession or purchase by person subject to   CRC 5.632

S

SUPREME COURT, CALIFORNIA
Chief Justice
Education of judicial branch
Bias, fairness and access, and the prevention of inappropriate workplace conduct   CRC 10.465
Justices
Education of judicial branch
Bias, fairness and access, and the prevention of inappropriate workplace conduct   CRC 10.465

T

TRANSLATORS AND INTERPRETERS
Court interpreters
Relay interpreters   CRC 2.893

TRIAL COURT, JUDICIAL BRANCH EDUCATION
Subordinate judicial officers
Bias, fairness and access, and the prevention of inappropriate workplace conduct   CRC 10.465

V

VIOLENCE PREVENTION
Workplace violence
Employer's action for injunctive relief to prevent   CRC 5.632

W

WORKPLACE VIOLENCE
Injunctive relief against violence or threat of violence toward employee   CRC 5.632